Lunarium

JOSEP LLUÍS AGUILÓ

Translated by
Anna Crowe

2016

Published by Arc Publications,
Nanholme Mill, Shaw Wood Road
Todmorden OL14 6DA, UK

978 1910345 46 7 (pbk)
978 1910345 47 4 (hbk)
978 1910345 48 1 (ebook)

Design by Tony Ward
Printed in Great Britain by T.J. International Ltd,
Padstow, Cornwall

Cover picture:
Fragment of watercolour 'Zobeida' from the *Invisible Cities* series
by Pedro Cano, by kind permission of the artist.

WITH THE SUPPORT OF:

Arc Publications 'Visible Poets' series
Series Editor: Jean Boase-Beier

CONTENTS

Josep Lluís Aguiló's fifth and latest collection, *Llunari*, which constitutes the bulk of this volume of translations, was published in 2008 and won the prestigious Premi Jocs Florals de Barcelona of that year. His previous collections are *Cants d'Arjau* (Songs from the Helm) 1986, *La biblioteca secreta* (The Secret Library) and *L'estació de les ombres* (The Season of Shadows), both in 2004. His collection *Monstres* (Monsters, 2005) was awarded the Premi Ciutat de Palma Joan Alcover Poetry Prize in 2005 and, in 2006, the National Critics' Prize for the best book of poems written in Catalan.

The epigraph, in which the poet sets out the various meanings of *Llunari* or *Lunarium* as given in the ten-volume Catalan-Valencian-Balear Dictionary of A. M. Alcover and F. de B. Moll, gives us a taste of where the book might take us: a preoccupation with time; books and magic, through which to predict the future or even summon up the devil; the body, and the lies that adults tell children in order to intimidate them. Already there is a sense that the reader may expect the unexpected. Reading these poems, what is striking is the power of the imagination at work, and the multiplicity of voices that speak through the poems. The power of the imagination might be said to be the underlying argument or leitmotif of Aguiló's poetry. There is a sense of the poet pushing the boundaries of the possible further and further out, of exploring what it means to live on the edge of whatever world he has invented, as well as, at the same time, going further and further in, exploring what it means to be human.

Like Pere Ballart, the editor of *Six Catalan Poets* (Arc Publications, 2013), I am reminded of the extraordinary fictions of Jorge Luís Borges, with whom Aguiló shares a predilection for myths and legends, for labyrinths, secret libraries, mirrors, the hermetic and the magical. In the opening poem, 'The Secret Library', Aguiló pays homage to Borges, the 'blind librarian', as well as to the great mediaeval Mallorcan writer, Ramon Llull, whom he pictures deciphering the pages of the natural world, that "*thicket of writing*, the green and yellow words / of chapters written by a botanical god." And yet, again like Borges, he is very much a poet of his own time, grounded in twenty-first century Spain, in particular the rural and maritime landscapes of the Balearics, and in everyday life, which he evokes in rich, sensuous language. The poetic voice can be humorous, tender, self-deprecating, but it also asks hard, uncomfortable questions and pulls no punches. The labyrinths and other worlds that Aguiló conjures up offer the perfect opportunity for examining our own world. The reader will here encounter pirates of the Caribbean, gunfighters of the wild west, fairies and fairytales, smugglers, hell and the devil, legends, and the world of the child. By offering the reader what is ostensibly another world to look at, the poet disarms us with strangeness until what is before us is suddenly all too familiar.

The voice in, for example, 'The Rules on Labyrinths', is that of a visionary who speaks with authority and precision, telling us he has written two rules on labyrinths in the narrow margins of the book of time. Why are the margins narrow, the reader wonders? We learn that the tunnels are to be made from 'the worn stone of days', and that the paths, which are obvious in spite of being covered with 'the vault of nights', lead ever further from the centre and are to be paved with 'dark desire'. We suddenly understand how brief our own lives are, how we waste time, and why those margins are so narrow. A strong moral sense, a sense of justice, runs like a vein through Aguiló's poetry, coming to the surface in poems like 'The Parasites of the Labyrinth', 'Prayer', 'The Just' and 'Waterloo', a long narrative poem that captures the lawlessness and terror of school, where tyranny and cruelty flourish unchecked and unpunished, and courage and loyalty go unrewarded.

The power of this poet's imagination finds marvellous expression in his poem, 'Heads or Tails'. Having decided that the head on the coin represents the masks we wear, and that the verso stands for the labyrinth, he then opts for a third and un-thought-of option, the edge:

> As for me, let me have the space occupied
> by the coin's edge, by its fields, cities
> and mountains. The eternal span of time
> where indecision reigns.

There is no value in any instant but that
which the coin impacts on, as it spins nimbly
on its profile, as vast as a world,
living, not having decided as yet
on which side it will have to lie down and die.

This superb piece of lateral thinking is not so much a call to rely on chance or fate, or to abdicate moral responsibility, as a call to live in the present; a joyful affirmation of the boundless power of the imagination, of life itself. This is lyrically sustained in another poem, 'The Attic', redolent with childhood memories of "the smells / of chicken bran and the dung and damp walls / of this corner of Santanyí and bad Mallorcan cement". The poet tells us that he still sneaks up there and sniffs for "the scent of moss, chicken-shit and old rushes". So effectively does he conjure up the sense of place both for himself and the reader that we share his astonishment when we come to the last line: "And I forget it's years since we demolished it." The power of the imagination can be harnessed to lead to self-knowledge, and one way of harnessing it is through writing, which can be seen as a kind of magic (or so, allegedly, we may read in *lunaria*), and this we are invited to do in a sparkling poem called 'The Ink Mirror'. In the pool of ink in your cupped palm you may see images of the future, but in that darkness is "a power it relinquishes from the first instant / that quill or nib is dipped in it." Out of this void and out of our own poverty, we are told, will come

the burning, desperate words
that, from the first instant you do so,
now and for ever more, like tatoos,
are a reflected image of yourself. Ink mirror, it's called.

Why not do it now? It's easy, it's magic.

The voice cajoles, we can hear the laughter in its words, but we remember that the truth burns and is desperate, as intimate as a tatoo, especially if it is "a reflected image of yourself". The mercurial shifts of tone are brilliantly handled, and there are many voices in this volume, where Aguiló speaks up for those who have no voice, and these come through in poems of great visual clarity, like 'The Guardians of the Frontier', which expands on a quotation from Robert Graves. Here the badly-paid soldiers, out on the wild edge of the country, rather like the characters of J. M Coetzee's novel, *Waiting for the Barbarians*, remind us that they

> ...earn the money you send us
> late and always grudgingly.
>
> We guard the lintel of the labyrinth
> of water, of earth, of stone and of flesh
> which is what frontiers are made of.
>
> Be alert, citizens: do not forget us;
> the wage is paltry; we owe you nothing.

It is worth contrasting the warning call of this underdog voice with the ashamed, skulking voice of 'The Parasites of the Labyrinth', those who have benefitted from the sins of the fathers and are prepared to go on doing so:

> We are its faithful heirs and its legacy,
> we hoard the gains yielded by centuries
> of this industry of genocide.

By writing this in the first person plural, Aguiló cunningly draws us in so that we find ourselves identifying with the voice of the poem, realising that we too are part of the conspiracy the first-world has gone on hatching throughout history. In his poem, 'Smuggling', the voice is an inhabitant of a remote, possibly third-world country which receives brief, sporadic visits and goods from a first-world bunch of smugglers. They bring these oppressed people "coffee-beans, spirits, penicillin / books that speak of things we know nothing about." But the smugglers betray their unwillingness really to engage with the tyranny the people suffer by refusing ever to land or even tie up while unloading the cargo, and the poem ends thus:

> They come and they go. They know they have to leave
> quickly to sail back along the return
> route to a place that doesn't exist;
> to a country where nothing is forbidden
> and where all the books are about us.

The poet exposes our own frequent unwillingness to engage

on a human level with oppression in other parts of the world, an oppression that we know all about through "all the books" at our disposal. No wonder, then, that those living under a tyrannous regime think of the freedom we have in the first world as happening in "a place that doesn't exist".

Perhaps the most extraordinary and terrifying poem in this collection, one which does indeed summon up the devil, as the epigraph warns us, is 'A Stay in Hell'. The voice of this poem is precise, informative and neutral, quietly charting the human gift for extraordinary cruelty which, Aguiló tells us, exceeds the skills of even the devil and his lesser demons:

> You people never fail to surprise us,
> your imagination reveals to us things
> that would never have occurred to a devil

I won't spoil the reader's enjoyment by revealing the ending.

Many of the poems in this collection are dark, exposing the worst that human nature is capable of, but this poet also writes warm and humane poems that dwell on the concerns of family life; even a dark poem like 'Genius Loci', which deals with mental illness within the family and the tragic damage done to personality by drug abuse, carries a charge of compassion, grief and kindness. 'Minerals' is touched by a father's pride in an eight-year-old, clever daughter who shares a passion for the truth and who will not be deceived by the false lures of magic or the labyrinth, and who shares his love of words, of the right words, the right names. Humour and affection also inform a poem like 'The Sea's Rules', full of sensuous, tactile imagery, where we learn that the poet and his brother used to share the annual chore of cleaning the hull of their sailing vessel with their bare hands. Now that technology has made the task easier, the poet is spared having to take part, freely admitting his own laziness and thanking his brother by acknowledging, by the end of the poem, that the boat has really become his brother's:

> He undoes his winter crustiness
> and washes his sores
> by robbing the keel of the dirt
> that slows down the thrust of his boat.

That self-deprecating note is found too in the humorous and affectionate account of how the poet acquired his three ancient Packards, for which he clearly feels a deep and superstitious affection (the poet being a collector of ancient cars). Aguiló is also a consummate love-poet, as we find in poems like 'Sweetheart', 'The Naming of Things', 'If This were a Fairy Tale' and 'Minimal Impacts'. This latter poem has at its heart the poignant image of a stone thrown into a pond by a soldier about to go into battle, ripples traveling out that perhaps cause him to draw

> conclusions on minimal effects;
> on the possible consequences
> of the impact of bullets on a body,
> on the impact of one love on the world.

I see the poems in this book as being like those ripples, traveling outwards, asking their hard questions, arriving with their extraordinary and beautiful images, and leaving us changed. Poetry, as Josep Lluís Aguiló says, in his poem of that name, is what is "left inside us / long after forgetting this poem".

Anna Crowe

LLUNARI *m*. 1. ant. Calendari en què s'indiquen les llunacions; cast. *lunario*. Item venut a Aloy steve un llunari, doc. a 1560 (arx parr. de Sta Col. de Q.). 2. Llibre màgic, on diuen que es poden llegir les prediccions de tot el que ha de succeir, i llegint-lo capgirat es pot fer sortir el dimoni i altres obres de bruixeria (mall.); cast. *lunario*. Treu un vell llunari... on llegia les males arts d'altre temps, tot enginy i bruixeria, tota llei d'encantaments, Colom Tres tar. 22 3. Taqueta blanca que es produeix dins l'ungla (Mall.). Els nins procuren no mostrar els llunaris que els han sortit, perquè, segons els diuen els majors, cada llunari indica una mentida que han dita. ETIM.: del llatí lunarium, derivat de luna.

A. M Alcover & F. De B. Moll
Diccionari Català-Valencià-Balear

LUNARIUM: 1. Arch. Calendar showing phases of the moon. Item sold to Aloy Steve, doc. in 1560 (parish archive of St Coloma de Queralt). 2. Book of magic in which, it is said, predictions may be read concerning everything that is to happen, while reading it upside-down may cause the devil and other works of witchcraft to appear (Mallorca); He pulls out an old lunarium... where he would read the wicked arts of other times, every devilment and wile, every rule on casting spells, Colom i Ferrà: The love of three oranges, 22. 3. Small white fleck produced under the fingernail (Mallorca). Children try to conceal any flecks that may have appeared, because, according to what grown-ups tell them, each fleck represents a lie they have told. ETYM.: from Latin lunarium, derived from luna: moon.

A. M Alcover & F. De B. Moll
Catalan-Valencian-Balear Dictionary

LES NORMES DELS LABERINTS

He escrit dues normes dels laberints
als marges estrets del llibre del temps.

La primera és que els seus túnels estiguin
fets de la pedra gastada dels dies
i coberts amb la volta de les nits.

La segona és que l'arquitecte etern
faci que els senders clars, inevitables,
els que ens facin anar més lluny del centre
tinguin el paviment de fosc desig.

THE RULES ON LABYRINTHS

I have written two rules on labyrinths
in the narrow margins of the book of time.

The first is that their tunnels should be
made of the worn stone of days
and covered with the vault of nights.

The second is that the everlasting architect
should make their clear, inevitable paths,
those that make us walk ever further from the centre,
to be paved with dark desire.

LES ROMPENTS DE L'INFINIT

Munti l'oreig que du l'escuma
de les rompents de l'infinit
JOAN ALCOVER, 'El Dol'

Les corrents ens portaven a la costa
com iots desarborats per la tempesta.
Cap a la riba, rere les rompents,
molt més enllà de qualsevol desig.

Estàvem oblidant les grapejades,
les succions, aquell moment convuls
en què cavalcàrem tot l'oceà
i tots els dies erms que ens esperaven.

Havíem perdut el significat
del que érem, ens havíem fragmentat,
ens havíem desclavat de les tatxes
que ens subjectaven i que ens explicaven
la carn salvatge que havíem sigut
i els llamps forcats que ens pertocaven ser.

Estàvem trencats. Després del desig
som anònims com restes d'un naufragi,
com branques trencades pel temporal,
com fragments de vidre polits pel mar.

INFINITY'S REEFS

Climb the storm that carries the foam
of infinity's reefs

JOAN ALCOVER, 'El Dol'

Currents carried us to the coast
like yachts dismasted by the storm.
As far as the shore, behind the reefs,
way beyond any desire.

We were forgetting the clawings,
the suctions, that convulsive moment
when we rode the entire ocean
and all the wild days awaiting us.

We had lost the sense
of what we were, we were fragmented,
we had yanked out the nails
that were pinning us and that explained to us
the wild flesh that we had been
and the forked lightning we were meant to be.

We were broken. When desire goes
we are anonymous as the flotsam from a wreck,
like branches broken by a gale,
like bits of glass polished by the sea.

A CARA O CREU

Què voleu que us digui? Cada cop més
penso que la cara i la creu abasten
territoris menors dels cobreixen
els traçats dels seus noms sobre la pàgina.

Sé que la cara és l'espai per a la màscara;
la creu és el signe del laberint.

A mi, deixau-me l'espai del cantell
de la moneda, els seus camps, ciutats
i muntanyes. El període etern
on senyoreja la indecisió.

No té valor cap altre instant que aquell
que la moneda impacta i àgil gira
sobre el seu perfil, immens com un món,
viva, sense haver decidit encara
de quin costat s'ha d'ajeure i morir.

HEADS OR TAILS

What do you want me to say? More and more
I think that the head, and the tail, on the coin,

embrace territories smaller than those covered
by the tracing of their names on the page.

I know that the head is the space for the mask;
the tail is the sign for the labyrinth.

As for me, let me have the space occupied
by the coin's edge, by its fields, cities
and mountains. The eternal period
where indecision reigns.

There is no value in any instant but that
which the coin impacts on, as it spins nimbly
on its profile, as vast as a world,
living, not having decided as yet
on which side it will have to lie down and die.

ELS GUARDIANS DE LA FRONTERA

We, not the city, are the empire's soul.

ROBERT GRAVES, 'The Cuirassiers of the Frontier

Envellim a la frontera esperant
que es decideixi d'un cop l'enemic.
Netejam les armes. Apuntalam
els parapets. Quan ve la fosca blava,
que és la frontera de la nit, bevem
els licors que ens preserven del temor
i del fred de les guàrdies nocturnes.

Nosaltres som les murades del regne;
els vostres molests bàrbars necessaris.

Som els últims guardians, davant nostre
s'obren les finestres i les escales;
les cruïlles i les portes del nord;
els comellars, els ponts i els aiguamolls;
els llindars, el bosc negre i els congosts.

Ens guanyam els diners que ens enviau
a deshora i sempre de mala gana.
Recordau que sense nosaltres, l'últim
reducte, la vostra primera línia,
pastura dels tigres, sense l'incòmoda
veritat que voldríeu amagar,
us desbordaríeu com llac sens riba,
us esfondraríeu com una casa
a la qual se li esbuquen les parets.

Fem guàrdia al dintell del laberint
d'aigua, de terra, de pedra i de carn
que és la substància de les fronteres.

Alertau ciutadans: no ens oblideu;
la soldada és poca; no us devem res.

THE GUARDIANS OF THE FRONTIER

We, not the city, are the empire's soul.
ROBERT GRAVES, 'The Cuirassiers of the Frontier'

We grow old at the frontier waiting
for the enemy suddenly to make a move.
We clean our weapons. We shore up
the parapets. With the coming of blue dusk,
which is the frontier of night, we drink
spirits to preserve us from the fear
and the cold of the night-watches.

We are the kingdom's ramparts;
your necessary troublesome barbarians.

We are the last guards, before us
windows and staircases open;
the crossroads and the gates to the north;
the watercourses, the bridges and the bogs;
the threshholds, the dark forest and the gorges.

We earn the money you send us
late and always grudgingly.
Remember that without us, the last
redoubt, your first line of defence,
tiger-bait, without the uncomfortable
truth that you would like to hide,
you would spill over like a lake with no shore,
you would collapse like a house
whose walls have been demolished.

We guard the lintel of the labyrinth
of water, of earth, of stone and of flesh
which is what frontiers are made of.

Be alert, citizens: do not forget us;
the wage is paltry; we owe you nothing.

PREGÀRIA

Tu bé ho saps, Senyor. Hem viscut just entre la posta
i la sortida del sol i mai no et buscarèm

quan sorpresos per l'adveniment de la nit
acatàvem el domini del seu imperi.

Tampoc quan buidàvem els vasos generosos,
mentre metabolitzàvem licor en coratge.

No t'hem necessitat ni en la conversa esparsa,
ni en l'últim cigarret manllevat de la nit,

Tu, Senyor, no eres als escusats quan rebíem
entre excrements, la comunió amb cocaïna

ni en les pistes de ball, talment camps de batalla,
on la promesa de sexe era l'única arma

i els moviments del ball un ritus d'agonia.
Ha anat bé, Senyor. Més que res no ens has fet nosa

ni tan sols quan, vençuts per les nits massa breus,
arrosegàvem els peus per túnels obscurs

de les sortides dels bars guiats per la llum
encegadora i hostil del portal del dia;

anant d'esma cap a la claror que ens tornava
a la tenebra de la diària mort.

PRAYER

How well you know it, Lord. We've lived merely between the setting
and the rising of the sun and never searched for you

when, surprised by the coming of night,
we revered the power of its dominion.

Nor when we drank down those generous glasses,
as we metabolized spirits into courage.

We had no need of you, either in our terse talk,
or in the final cigarette borrowed from the night.

You, Lord, were not in the lavatory when we received,
among excrements, the communion with cocaine

nor on the dance-floors, just like battlefields,
where the promise of sex was the only weapon

and the dance movements a rite of agony.
It's gone well, Lord. Above all, you've never bothered us

not even when, beaten by nights that were too short,
we dragged our feet through the dark tunnels

of the exits from bars guided by the blinding
and hostile light of the gate of day;

from instinct going towards the brightness that sent us
back to the gloom of daily death.

ELS PARÀSITS DEL LABERINT

Som els seus hereus, vivim de la deixa.
Estimam el que en resta. Estimam
les seves dèries, la impaciència,
els llibres repetits, les cases velles.

Som els paràsits d'aquest laberint.
Estimam la sang seca a les parets,
les taques grogues dels llençols, els cruis
del sostre i els racons amb teranyines.

En som els hereus fidels i la deixa,
atresoram els guanys retuts pels segles
d'aquesta indústria del genocidi.

Giram cara a la paret certs retrats
de la nostra avior. En dormim els somnis.
N'estimam, sobretot, les grans excuses.

THE PARASITES OF THE LABYRINTH

We are its heirs, we live off the legacy.
We cherish what's left of it. We cherish
its manias, the impatience,
the multiple copies of books, the old houses.

We are the parasites of this labyrinth.
We cherish the dried blood on its walls,
the yellow stains on the sheets, the cracks
in the ceiling and the corners hung with cobwebs.

We are its faithful heirs and its legacy,
we hoard the gains yielded by centuries
of this industry of genocide.

We turn to the wall certain portraits
of our ancestry. We put their dreams to sleep.
We cherish, more than anything, huge excuses.

ELS JUSTS

Segons tradicions jueves
viuen ocults entre nosaltres:
Són els trenta-sis homes justs
que suporten el pes del món.

També en parla l'Islam: el món
continua existint perquè
hi ha quaranta homes, els Abdals,
que infatigables ne s'ocupen.

Visc a una illa al mig del Mediterrani,
aquí la salvació de tots és
feina de tres pilars d'or que suporten
el pes d'una muntanya que es diu Randa.

Dels tres pilars n'hi ha dos ja trencats
i un de cruiat. Quan l'esforç l'espatlli,
aquesta illa, que és el món, morirà
com una Atlàntida, sota les aïgues.

Cada poble necessita posar
la responsabilitat de la seva
pervivència en les mans més segures.

Els illencs sabem que mai no es podrà
confiar en la solidesa dels homes
i que si hem de posar el nostre destí
en mans d'altri, perquè així són les normes,
confiarem abans en l'or trencat
que en la pretesa integritat dels justs.

THE JUST

According to Jewish tradition
they live hidden in our midst:
they are the thirty-six just men
who bear the weight of the world.

Islam too speaks of them; the world
goes on existing because
there are forty men, the Abdals,
who tirelessly take care of it.

I live on an island in the middle of the Mediterranean,
where the salvation of all
is the work of three gold pillars that support
the weight of a mountain called Randa.

Of the three pillars two are already broken
and one is cracked. When strain splits it apart,
this island, which is the world, will perish
beneath the waters, like an Atlantis.

Every nation needs to place
the responsibility for their
survival in the safest hands.

We islanders know that you can never
rely on men to stand firm
and that if we have to place our future
in the hands of others, since these are the rules,
we will place our trust in broken gold
before the vaunted integrity of the just..

LA ROCA NEGRA

Et vares enrolar en la *Roca Negra*
i prest en vares ser el capità.

Vares lluitar, capturares vaixells,
sepultares tresors i gent.

Navegares els cossos de les filles
de tots els virreis del Carib
(aquesta és una manera romàntica
de dir el que realment vares fer).

Sempre et creies que eres a punt
de viure el que havia de ser
l'aventura més extraordinària.

Perderes la mà i et va nèixer un garfi
al monyó i vares a començar
a perseguir en Peter, de dia i nit,
com un malalt, de manera obsessiva.

Un dia et vares adonar
que estaves perdent massa temps
fugint d'un cocodril inversemblant
que portava un rellotge al ventre.

THE BLACK ROCK

You joined the crew of the *Black Rock*
and soon you were the captain.

You fought, you captured ships,
you buried treasures and people.

You sailed across the bodies of daughters
of all the viceroys in the Caribbean
(this is a romantic way
of saying what you really did).

You always believed you were on the point
of living what was bound to be
the most extraordinary adventure.

You lost a hand and a claw grew
on the stump and you started
to persecute Peter, day and night,
like a sick man, obsessively.

One day you realised
you were losing too much time
running away from an unlikely crocodile
that carried a clock in its belly.

HE PERDUT ALGUNS VERSOS

L'àngel de la canalla
vindrà de grat amb una
delegació dels seus.

Bartomeu Fiol, 'Canalla lluny de Grècia'

Són com animals esquius,
a cops se'm passegen per sobre
o se m'esmunyen entre els peus
i em fan ensopegar.

N'he caçat sovint en l'última revinglada,
en els moviments més convulsos de l'amor;
després, endormiscat, he mig obert la mà
i han escapat d'entre els dits, com insectes.

També n'he perdut per mandra
de llevar-me del llit;
si els enganxo a un paper
sovint acaben diluïts
en el sabó de la bugada.

O els ha espatllat l'esperit d'un licor,
una visita que venia de Porlock,
la urgència de l'últim cigarret
o els viatges imprevists al banc.

A moments em pensava
que la memòria, l'amant voluble
que no pot evitar trair-me,
els subjectava i no els deixava anar.

Com sempre, m'equivocava,
descurada com és, els va deixar
a l'abast de l'oblit.

I HAVE LOST A FEW LINES

The angel of the mob
will willingly come with a
delegation of his own.
BARTOLOMEU FIOL "The mob a long way from Greece"

They are like shy animals,
sometimes they pass right over me
or glide between my feet
and trip me up.

I have often chased them in the final spasm,
in the most convulsive movements of love-making;
later, dozing, I have half-opened my hand
and they escaped from between my fingers, like insects.

Some I have lost through idleness,
failing to get up from my bed;
if I pin them down on paper
they often end up diluted
by the soap in the washing-machine.

Or some spiritous liquor has ruined them,
or the visitor from Porlock,
or the need for a last cigarette
or unforeseen trips to the bank.

At times I have thought
that memory, that voluble lover
that cannot help but betray me,
was holding them and would not let them go.

As ever, I was wrong,
for being careless, she had left them
where oblivion could reach them.

El pitjor és que sóc conscient
que els versos fugitius
se'n van a un poema que rellegeixo
sovint al mig de la nit, i que no puc recordar
quan em treu del llit, amb la llum de l'alba,
la bóta de ferro del dia.

The worst of it is, I'm aware
that those fugitive lines
went into a poem I read again
often in the middle of the night, a poem I can't recall
when I'm kicked out of bed, with the light of dawn,
by the iron boot of day.

TUMBLEWEED

Quantos Césares fui!

Fernando Pessoa-Álvaro de Campos, 'Pecado Original'

Les seves mans esperen als revòlvers.
No deixa cap ombra el sol del migdia.

L'enemic està només a vint passes.
La imatge del duel es repeteix:
és l'enèsim encontre de la mà
amb el ferro modelat, per enèsima
vegada, amb una de les formes noves
que l'enginy ens permet donar a la mort.

La pols del carrer els ha cobert les botes,
els espectadors esperen el tret,
el saloon ha despatxat esperit
de fusta mesclat amb verí de serp.

Fa sols tres dies que cavalquen junts.
Ara fa mesos que no s'han banyat.
Fa tres dies que esperen el moment
de l'explosió que alliberarà
una bala del seu catau de bronze.

Un d'ells porta al coll un amulet indi
(com és que el té és una altra història).
Un no ha matat mai ningú per l'esquena.
Un, mai no s'ha sentit tan viu com ara.

Un d'ells va deixar una dona i dos fills;
fa dos anys que no els ha enviat diners.
Un d'ells morirà d'aquí a uns instants
però jo no m'havia sentit mai
la meitat de viu de com em sent ara.

TUMBLEWEED

I was so many Caesars!
FERNANDO PESSOA-ALVARO DE CAMPOS, 'Original Sin'

Their hands are poised on their revolvers.
The midday sun casts no shadow.

The enemy is only twenty paces away.
The image of the duel repeats itself:
it is the umpteenth meeting between hand
and pressed metal, for the umpteenth
time, with one of the novel shapes
that ingenuity allows us to give death.

The dust of the street has covered their boots,
the spectators are waiting for the shot,
the saloon has sold liquor made from
wood alcohol mixed with snake-poison.

It's only three days they've ridden together.
Now it's months since they took a bath.
For three days they have been waiting
for the moment of the explosion that will free
a bullet from its bronze lair.
One of them wears round his neck an Indian charm
(how he happens to have it is another story).
One of them has never shot a man in the back.
One of them has never felt so alive as he does now.

One of them left behind a wife and two children;
it's two years since he sent them any money.
One of them will die in just a few moments
but I have never felt
half as alive as I do now.

LECTOR

El primer vers és la porta que t'obre
la casa del poema. El que convida
a entrar i a posar-t'hi còmode.
La primera estrofa és la que et dóna
la benvinguda i t'arrossega a dins,
agafant-te pel braç i arrufant-se contra tu;
la que et parla de calor i confiança
alhora que et fa seure a la butaca de la segona estrofa.

On has d'esperar que el sentit del poema
et porti un cafè, calent i dolç, per dar-te
alguna cosa perquè tinguis les mans
ocupades i no puguis desviar l'atenció
o agafar un diari del revister.

Ben aviat entrarà la conclusió
per la porta del darrere,
silenciosament i de puntes,
mentre el volum de la música augmenta
i és quan, per fi, intueixes que tothom
ja sap si la mà que amaga a l'esquena
porta una carta d'amor
o un punyal.

READER

The first line is the door that opens for you
the house of the poem. The one that invites you
to come in and make yourself comfortable.
The first stanza is the one that welcomes
you and drags you inside,
grabbing you by the arm and frowning at you;
the one that speaks to you with warmth and trust
while it makes you sit down in the armchair of the second stanza.

Where you have to wait for the meaning of the poem
to bring you a coffee, hot and sweet, to give you
something so as to make sure your hands
are occupied and you don't lose concentration
or pick up a newspaper from the rack.

Soon the conclusion will arrive
through the back door,
silently and on tiptoe,
while the volume of the music rises
and this is when, at last, you intuit that everyone
already knows whether the hand hidden behind his back
holds a love-letter
or a dagger.

UNA TEMPORADA A L'INFERN

Com que era un artista en la seva professió,
quan va arribar a l'infern el feren passar a una sala
luxosa i es va asseure al sofà amb el que manava.

– Les seves habilitats – li va dir – no es poden perdre.
Un home amb la teva experiència és valuós
per a nosaltres, i el teu art ens pot ajudar
a aprendre maneres millors de fer la nostra feina.

Durant l'eternitat es va dedicar a aplicar dolor
en totes les seves formes, Va aconseguir arribar
al virtuosisme, al comneixement exacte del
nervis del cos i de l'ànima i va aprendre
que l'eina que produia el màxim efecte
era la que feia palanca en l'esperança.

Tenia espectadors que prenien notes,
aprenents i dimonis menors,
les seves arts canviaren els usos i costums
de l'infern; va fer renéixer la passió pel càstig
en dimonis desmotivats per la cruel eternitat.

Les ànimes que passavenper les seves mans
eren variades: nins, joves, homes vells
que reberen les atencions del seu art
i serviren perquè el seu mestratge
atenyés la ribera de la perfecció.

El dia assenyalat com la fi de l'eternitat
el va enviar a demanar el seu cap
i el va tornar a fer asseure al sofà i li digué:
– Estem satisfets de tu, has arribat als cims
de la teva professió, és l'hora d'un ascens.

A STAY IN HELL

As he was an artist by profession,
when he arrived in hell he was taken to a luxurious
chamber and sat down on a sofa beside his guide.

– Your skills – he was told – must not be lost.
A man with your experience is of great value
to us, and your art can assist us
in learning better ways of doing our job.

Through eternity he dedicated himself to applying pain
in all its forms. He reached a level of
virtuosity, a knowledge of the precise
nerves of the body and of the soul, and he learned
that the tool that produced the maximum effect
was the one that used a lever on hope.

He had spectators taking notes,
apprentices and lesser demons,
his arts changed the uses and habits
of hell; he caused a revival in the passion for punishment
in demons demotivated by cruel eternity.

The souls that passed through his hands
were various: children, young people, old men
who received the attentions of his art
and served their turn that his mastery
might attain the zenith of perfection.

On the day appointed as the end of eternity
he was summoned by the leader,
who led him back to the sofa and said to him:
– We are pleased with you, you have reached the heights
of your profession, it is time for a promotion.

– No cal – va dir, modest, però el Diable
va insistir tot dient – Sempre ens sorpreneu,
la vostra imaginació ens descobreix coses
que ni se li haguessin acudit a un diable
– i amb un gest elegant li llevà la bena dels ulls
i a l'instant va poder recordar
que totes les ànimes amb les quals havia treballat
portaven variacions de la seva cara
i que les súpliques li anaven dirigides pel seu nom,
i que l'eternitat just acabava de començar,
mentre se l'emprtaven on
s'esperava ell mateix amb els ulls embenats.

– There is no need – he said, modestly, but the Devil
insisted, saying – You people never fail to surprise us,
your imagination reveals to us things
that would never have occurred to a devil
– and with an elegant gesture he lifted the blindfold from his eyes
and in that instant he was able to remember
that all the souls with whom he had worked
had variations of his own face
and that their supplications were addressed to him by name,
and that eternity had only just begun,
while they carried him off to where
his blindfolded self was waiting for him.

GUINEU

Com a bon espartà suportes
les ferides sense voler adonar-te
que el vigilant ho sap.

Segurament, està jugant amb tu.

Els dos sabeu que el delicte
no és que l'hagis robada,
sinó que t'agafin.

I ben mirar és una bajanada
ser tan espartà que no puguis
obrir el sobre, mirar l'anàlisi
i saber si has d'anar al metge
a treure't la guineu del ventre.

FOX

Like a good Spartan you put up with
the wounds without wanting to realise
that the warder knows all about it.

He is playing with you, for sure.

Both of you know that the crime
is not that you stole it,
but that you've been caught.

And looked at clearly it's a piece of idiocy
to be such a Spartan that you cannot
open the envelope, read the results of the tests
and know whether you have to go to the doctor
to have the fox removed from your stomach.

EL CONTRACTE

A cada cop el clau s'enfonsa més
en la peülla i el ferrador en corregeix
la inclinació amb martellades laterals.

A cada cop de l'home contra l'unglot
el cavall s'estremeix.
Només el costum el fa restar immòbil.
És el costum. La seva sang no recorda
haver estat un poltre entre iurtes mongols;
haver flanquejat les falanges d'Alexandre;
les càrregues en què ha mossegat i pegat coces.

La seva pell no recorda el llim del Nil
ni les arenes d'Aràbia,
no pot recordar els carretons i les caravanes,
ni la visió d'un ramat d'egües vora un llac.

Ell no sap res del so de les petjades
dels soldats darrere seu. Als cascs
no ha conegut el terra de granit
d'un Arc de Triomf i no l'ha escalfat
el marbre calent d'Hagia Sophia en flames.

Els cops rítmics del martell del ferrador
no li serveixen per fer memòria
del colpejar contra el flanc de la motxilla
del pony express, la seva boca no recorda
les llagues de l'embocadura, els esperons als flancs;
ni la suor recompensada pel triomf
ni les fuetades que són filles de les curses perdudes.

THE CONTRACT

With each blow the nail is driven deeper
into the hoof and the blacksmith corrects
the angle with sideways blows of the hammer.

With each blow the man makes against the hoof
the horse shudders.
Only habit makes it keep still.
It is habit. Its blood holds no memory
of having been a foal among mongol yurts;
of having flanked the phalanxes of Alexander;
the charges where it bit and kicked.

Its hide does not remember the mud of the Nile
or the sands of Arabia,
it cannot remember the carts and caravans,
nor the vision of a herd of mares beside a lake.

It knows nothing of the sound of tramping
soldiers behind it. Under its hooves
it has not known the granite rock
of a Triumphal Arch and has not been scorched
by the hot marble of Hagia Sofia in flames.

The blacksmith's rhythmic hammer-blows
in no way help it to remember
the way the saddlebag of the pony-express
would bang against its flank, its mouth does not recall
the sores the bit made, the spurs in its flanks;
nor its sweat rewarded by victory
or the whippings that are the offspring of races lost.

Cada ferradura és un contracte en semicercle
que renovam periòdicament i que diu:
a cops t'estimo, sempre et necessito,
porta't bé; potser fruiràs la misericòrdia
d'una bala i potser, quan siguis vell,
fins i tot esdevindràs carn.

Every horseshoe is a semicircular contract
that we renew regularly and which says:
sometimes we love you, we always have need of you,
behave well; perhaps you will be granted the mercy
of a bullet and maybe, when you are old,
you will even become meat.

ESTÀTICA

No t'ho dic per res, però crec
que convé que tenguis en compte
que hi ha una possibilitat
que moris sol,
amb els calçons cagats,
i que al teu cadàver,
enmortallat amb vòmit i sang,
sols el vetlli l'estàtica del televisor.

STATIC

I'm not telling you this for any particular reason,
but I think you should take into account
that there is a possibility
that you may die alone,
having shit yourself,
and that your dead body,
shrouded in vomit and blood,
may have as its only wake the static on the television.

ELS DRETS DELS MORTS

Tenen els seus sindicats. S'ajunten
en associacions per establir
els seus drets i preferències.

N'hi ha alguns que s'estimen més
la cremació i que els seus cossos
esdevinguin cendra i fum.

D'altres prefereixen la permanència
dels taüts enterrats i d'altres
reclamen ser esquarterats a les altes
muntanyes perquè les aus
els devorin i, així, formar part del vent.

També a cops els morts ens demanen
alguna venjança i que ens alegrem
de la mort dels seus enemics
o dels triomfs de la seva nissaga.

Les agrupacions es pleguen a les modes
dels seus membres i ens diuen
als vius a l'orella que obeïm els precs
dels que, absents, ens exigeixen
que tinguem presents els seus drets
i, si podem, que lluitem les seves guerres.

Així els morts no se sentiran tan lluny
i es conformaran amb les seves peticions
puerils quan tornin a poder comprovar
que mai no podrem suportar la seva absència.

THE RIGHTS OF THE DEAD

They have their trade unions. They unite
in associations to establish
their rights and preferences.

There are some who would rather
be cremated and have their bodies
become ash and smoke.

Others prefer the permanence
of buried coffins and yet others
demand to be quartered and placed on high
mountains so that birds may devour them
and thus become part of the wind.

At times, too, the dead demand of us
vengeance and that we should rejoice
in the death of their enemies
or in the triumphs of their lineage.

The groups shape themselves to the styles
of their members and whisper in the ears
of us, the living, that we should obey the prayers
of those who, though absent, require us
ever to bear in mind their rights
and, if we can, to fight their wars.

And thus the dead won't feel so far away
and will resign themselves with their childish
petitions when they attempt to prove again
that we'll never be able to bear their absence.

AMIGA

Ara que ha acabat la nit i has marxat
i que t'he vist, tan bella i tan cansada,
pens que t'hauria d'haver dit que mai
no tornarem ser tan joves com ara.

Ens ofegam en una mar de temps.
Demà serem més vells. Potser pus mai
no posseirem l'energia exacta
per muntar la nit el cos de l'altre.

La nostra amistat no ha sigut gens fàcil;
no ens hem mentit més que quan ens hem dit
que el desig no hi tenia res a veure.

Per res voldria fer que s'acabés
la nostra relació; tan perfecta
que als dos ens conformam a cimentar-la
en la suposició que pus mai
acabam les nostres nits al teu llit.

SWEETHEART

Now that the night is over and you have left
and that I have seen you, so beautiful and so tired,
I think that I should have told you that never
will we go back to being as young as now.

We are drowning in a sea of time.
Tomorrow we will be older. Maybe we'll never
again have the energy needed
to make love with the night on each other's body.

Our friendship has not been at all easy;
we've never lied more than when we told each other
that desire had nothing to do with it.

I wouldn't want our relationship to end,
not for all the world; so perfect
that both of us agree in cementing it
by the supposition that never more
should we end our nights in your bed.

LES METÀFORES DE LA NOSTRA EDAT

Les Onades, les gleves de petroli,
el fum de les explosions, el foc
negre, la llum incerta, la pistola
ceràmica, tots els femers farcits
de nosaltres, l'òrfena cara de llauna,
l'electrònica devastada, els cables
de color tallats, el teu sexe eixut,
la cara esclafada al vidre del cotxe,
els tumors interns i externs, el fibló,
la derrota, la mar extenuada.

Les metàstasis de l'apocalipsi.

METAPHORS FOR OUR AGE

The Tsunamis, the oil-spills,
the smoke from explosions, the black
fire, the doubtful light, the ceramic
gun, all the dung-heaps stuffed
with ourselves, the tinned meat of unknown parentage,
the electronics devastated, the coloured cables
severed, your dry vagina,
the face crushed against the windscreen,
tumours within and without, the tornado,
the defeat, the exhausted sea.

The metastases of the apocalypse.

És màgia, és fàcil, ara ho pots fer.
Es diu, als llunaris, mirall de tinta.
Es posa tinta al recipient còncau
que es fa arrufant el pamell de la mà.
Si t'hi concentres s'hi veuen passar
l'esquelet del món, el cavall salvatge,
el dèdal al creu de la moneda,
el tresor ocult i la mort del just.

Si un dia et canses de només mirar
els misteris que t'ofrena el mirall
podràs utilitzar la seva màgia
i amollar tot el poder que reté
la seva superba obscuritat nua
i que allibera des del primer cop
que va mullar-s'hi una ploma o un estil.

El poder hipnòtic que et força a observar
dins de la teva pròpia misèria
i a pintar en el buit que t'ha estat donat
les paroles ardents, desesperades,
que, d'ença del primer moment que ho fas,
ara i per sempre més, com tatuages,
t'enmirallen. Es diu mirall de tinta.

Per què no ho fas ara? És fàcil, és màgia.

THE MIRROR OF INK

It's magic, it's easy, you can do it now.
In *lunaria* it's called an ink mirror.
You pour ink into the hollow
made by cupping the palm of your hand.
If you stare into it you can see passing across it
the skeleton of the world, the wild horse,
the maze on the reverse of the coin,
the buried treasure-hoard and the death of the just man.

If one day you tire of simply gazing
at the mysteries the mirror gives you
you'll be able to use its magic
to tame all the power held
by its proud bare darkness,
a power it hands over from the first instant
that a quill or a nib was dipped in it.

The hypnotic power that forces you to observe
within your own poverty
and to paint, in the void that has been given you,
the burning, desperate words
that, from the first instant you do so,
now and for ever more, like tatoos,
mirror yourself. Ink mirror, it's called.

Why not do it now? It's easy, it's magic.

TRES PACKARDS

Ask The Man Who Owns One
Lema de la Packard Motor Car Company, 1899-1957

i Touring

It's a lean car… a long-legged dog of a car… a gray-ghost eagle car.
The feet of it eat the dirt of a road… the wings of it eat the hills.
Danny the driver dreams of it when he sees women in red skirts and red sox in his sleep.
It is in Danny's life and runs in the blood of him… a lean gray-ghost car.
Carl Sandburg, 'Portrait of a Motor Car'

El primer Packard que va arribar a casa,
un descapotable de sis cilindres,
fabricat el mil nou-cents vint-quatre,
va renéixer d'entre un núvol de pols
quan el desvestiren de les mantes
que l'amagaven en la cotxeria
on feia anys que s'anava rovellant.
Va ser com descobrir una Afrodita
de marbre enterrada en un pou de fang.

Despullaren la bellesa damnada
i veren com s'anava vestint amb
les protestes del seu propietari,
un arquitecte vell i malcarat.
– No me'l vull vendre
– afirmava enfadat,
mentre el tumor, encovat al seu cap,
li estenia els tentacles pel futur.

THREE PACKARDS

Ask The Man Who Owns One

MOTTO OF THE PACKARD MOTOR CAR COMPANY, 1899-1957

I TOURING

It's a lean car… a long-legged dog of a car… a gray-ghost eagle car.
The feet of it eat the dirt of a road… the wings of it eat the hills.
Danny the driver dreams of it when he sees women in red skirts and red sox in his sleep.
It is in Danny's life and runs in the blood of him… a lean gray-ghost car.

CARL SANDBURG, 'Portrait of a Motor Car'

The first Packard that entered the house,
a six-cylinder touring
built in nineteen twenty-four,
was re-born in a cloud of dust
when they stripped away the travel-rugs
that were concealing it in the coach-house
where it had been rusting away for years.
It was like discovering a marble
Aphrodite at the bottom of a muddy pond.
They laid bare that condemned beauty
and saw how it was being clothed
in the protests of its owner,
an old and surly architect.
– I don't want to sell it
– he declared crossly,
while the tumour squatting in his brain
spread its tentacles out into the future.

II CONVERTIBLE SEDAN

él examina un coche muchísimo más caro
– un Duesenberg sport con doble parabrisas,
bello como una máquina de guerra –
JAIME GIL DE BIEDMA 'Barcelona ja no és bona...'

El segon: un vuit cilindres del vint-
i-nou. El va anar a negociar a Tucson.
És un convertible, de quatre portes,
fet per Ray Dietrich just després de vendre
Le Baron Carrossiers, fart d'haver
de fingir accent francès als seus clients.

– El clima del desert és el millor
pels cotxes – li deia el propietari,
un polonès amb aspecte d'actor
de cinema, mentre la seva dona
li feia l'ullet i l'encanonaven
dos pits espectaculars, impossibles;
puntals i senyera de l'avançada
indústria estètica del país.

– Surt a una pel·lícula de Blake Edwards
– li contava provant d'enlluernar-lo.

II Convertible Sedan

he examines a much more expensive vehicle
– a Duesemberg sportscar with double windscreen,
beautiful as a war-machine –
Jaime Gil de Biedma 'Barcelona's no longer any good…'

The second: a nineteen twenty-nine eight-cylinder.
He went to bargain for it in Tucson.
It's a convertible with four doors,
made by Ray Dietrich just after he had sold
Le Baron Carrossiers, sick of having
to fake a French accent for his customers.

– The desert climate is the best
for cars – the proprietor was telling him,
a Pole who looked like a cinema actor,
while his wife made eyes at him
and aimed two spectacular, impossible
breasts at him; the pillars
and banners of the advanced
aesthetic industry of the country.

– It appears in a Blake Edwards film –
the guy said, trying to dazzle him.

III Convertible Victoria

De matí em plau, amb fèrries tenalles
i claus de tub, cercar la peça llosca
a l'embragat, o al coixinet que embosca
l'eix, i engegar per l'asfalt sense falles.

J. V. Foix, 'Sol i de dol'

El tercer també va ser un convertible,
un vuit cilindres del trenta-quatre
amb culata d'alta compressió,
li va portar Jean-François du Montand;
marchand francès expansiu i xerraire.

Li deia que l'havia restaurat
a París un germà del Xa de Pèrsia.

Du Montand va morir molt poc després,
atropellat i esclafat per un cotxe,
quan estava sortint d'un restaurant
on havia sopat per celebrar
finalment la compra d'un Delage a una
vídua gasiva i recalcitrant.

Mai ha volgut esbrinar si tenia
efectivament algun germà el Xa.

iii Convertible Victoria

In the morning, what I like to do, armed
with steel pliers and tubular spanners, is search for the
dodgy piece in the coupling, or in the bearing that ambushes
the axle, then get going along the asphalt with never a break-down.
J. V. Foix, 'Alone and in mourning'

The third was likewise a convertible,
a nineteen thirty-four eight-cylinder
with high-compression cylinder-head,
brought to him by Jean-François du Montand;
an expansive and talkative French marchand.

He told him it had been restored in Paris
by a brother of the Shah of Persia.

Du Montand died very shortly afterwards,
knocked down and run over by a car,
when he was leaving a restaurant
where he had had dinner to celebrate
finally buying a Delage from
a stingy and recalcitrant widow.

He has never wanted to find out
whether the Shah really did have a brother.

EL NOM DE LES COSES

És la primera feina que ens manà
un déu de venjança. Un creador
poc hàbil al qual se li revoltaven
els àngels i a qui no creien les dones.

Només això: posam nom a les coses.
Això és el que feim d'ençà del principi.

Ho hem anat fentel millor que sabem
i, com taxonomistes obsessius,
morim alegres per un nom de lloc
o per decidir el nom d'un déu inútil.

Hi va haver moments que passava pena
de defallir buscant noms vertaders
per a la suma de coses que ets:
carn, ivori, safirs, ulls, alè, ambre.

Ara no en passo, he arribat sense por
a la trinxera des d'on es comprèn
que tot nom és bo per a tota cosa
i que el món mereix un nom només
perquè puc recordar que tu hi vius.

THE NAME OF THINGS

It is the first task we were ordered to carry out
by a vengeful god. A clumsy
creator whose angels revolted against him
and whom women did not obey.

Just this: we must name things.
This is what we do from the very beginning.

We have gone on doing it as well as we know how
and, like obsessive taxonomists,
we die made happy by a place-name
or by deciding on the name of a useless god.

There were moments when I was terrified
of dying while searching for the true names
for the sum of the things you are:
flesh, ivory, sapphires, eyes, breath, amber.

This no longer happens, I have come fearlessly
to the trench where one clearly understands
that every name is good for everything
and that the world deserves a name simply
because I can remember that you live in it.

EL CONTRABAN

Els contrabandistes vénen d'enfora
seguint estels de claror il·legal.

Ens porten de molt lluny, amb el vaixell,
fil de seda, tabac de picadura,
grans de cafè, licors, penicil·lina,
llibres que parlen del que no sabem.

La seva feina és mirar l'espadat
de la costa i buscar entre la fosca
els camins que apareixen a la nit
fets amb la llum dels fanals de carbur.

Vetllen com es descarrega el viatge
i frisen per deslliurar-se del gènere.
Llests per partir, sols no llancen mai l'àncora
ni fermen la barca a cap penyal.

Vénen i s'en van. Saben que han d'anar-se'n
aviat per navegar pel camí
de tornada a un lloc que no existeix;
a un país on res no està prohibit
i on tots els llibres parlen de nosaltres.

SMUGGLING

The smugglers come from elsewhere
following comets of illegal brightness.

They bring us from far away, in their vessel,
silk thread, loose tobacco,
coffee-beans, spirits, penicillin,
books that speak of things we know nothing about.

Their task is to search the cliffs
of the coast and peer through the darkness
for the paths that are visible at night
strung with the light from carbide lamps.

They watch over how the voyage is discharged
and fret to be rid of their cargo.
Eager to leave, they simply never drop anchor
nor moor the ship to any rock.

They come and they go. They know they have to leave
quickly to sail back along the return
route to a place that doesn't exist;
to a country where nothing is forbidden
and where all the books speak about us.

TENIM UNA CASA A LA PLATJA

Aquesta casa està davant la platja
i cada cop que sortim pel portal
els nostres peus s'endinsen en la sorra.

D'un temps ençà s'ha trobat submergida
sota altres cases, que l'han ofegat
sense pietat, per tots els costats.

Amb el temps, entre la casa i la platja
s'han anat bastint altres edificis
on viu gent que no coneix ni saluda
i s'han instal·lat tendes de records
i hotels des d'on molts de desconeguts
es miren la platja sense saber
que no poden apropar-s'hi, que és nostra.

Que quan sortim cada dia al carrer
es fonen l'asfalt i la voravia
i els nostres peus s'endinsen en la sorra.

La casa està separada només
del coster per la distància elàstica
que deixam que ens separi l'un de l'altre.

WE HAVE A HOUSE BESIDE THE BEACH

This house faces the beach
and each time we go out of the door
our feet sink into the sand.

For some time now it has become submerged
beneath other houses that have stifled it
remorselessly, on every side.

With time, between the house and the beach
they have gone on putting up other buildings
where people live who neither know us nor offer any greeting
and they've installed souvenir shops
and hotels from which lots of strangers
gaze at the beach without knowing
that they cannot come near it, that it's ours.

That every day when we go out into the street
the asphalt and the pavement melt
and our feet sink into the sand.

The house is separated from the shore
only by the elastic distance
we allow to separate us one from the other.

LES NORMES DE LA MAR

Cada primavera s'han de treure les barques
de la mar i deixar-les assecar.

La fusta desprèn l'aigua de l'hivern
i les quilles apareixen enfundades de pedra
quan se'ls eixuga la crosta inevitable
d'algues, crustacis i anemones.

Fins fa poc, cada primavera,
amb el meu germà, rascàvem la quilla,
fins a la fusta, amb espàtules.

Arrabassàvem els cargols, les pegellides
i tota la munió de paràsits
que frenaria l'avanç de la barca.
D¡aquesta manera navegaríem
la promesa d'un mar que es diria l'estiu.

Li netejàvem la pell al vaixell
i ens feríem les man i les ungles
contra les agrupacions calcàries
que, com carenes o runes minúscules,
haviem obrat un diorama a l'obra viva.

Fèiem poca planta; cremats
pel primer sol, amb les samarretes
plenes de pols blanca i pintura
i les mans nafrades, tacades
del betum que segreguen les algues.

THE SEA'S RULES

Every spring the boats have to be hauled
out of the sea and left to dry.

The wood releases the water of winter
and the hull appears to be sheathed in stone
when we begin removing the inevitable crust
of sea-weed, crustaceans and anemones.

Until recently, every spring,
my brother and I would scour the keel
down to the wood with paint scrapers.

We hacked away the whelks, the limpets
and the whole mass of parasites
that would slow down the forward thrust of the boat.
In this way we'd sail
the promise of a sea that would be called summer.

We cleaned the skin of the boat
and we damaged our hands and nails
on the chalky incrustations
which, like ridges or minute ruins,
had created a diorama on the hull.

We weren't much to look at; burned
by the early sun, our T-shirts
thick with white dust and paint
and our hands hacked, stained
by the bitumen that sea-weed secretes.

Fa uns anys que per fer el mateix
empram llances d'aigua a pressió
que desprenen aquestes colònies
de manera còmoda i a distància,
sense haver d'esgarrinxar-nos les mans.
L'aigua que els va donar vida
arrabassa les seves despulles
amb violència impersonal.

Ara, gairebé sempre, fa aquesta feina el meu germà:
és més voluntariós, i estima fer feina
amb les mans, sobretot si és a la barca.

Ell, per tot l'amor que em té,
m'estalvia la incomoditat
de trair la meva mandra,

Es desfà de la seva crostera d'hivern
i es neteja la nafra
arrabassant la brutor de la quilla
que detura l'avanç de la seva barca.

For some years now, to do the same job
we use pressure washers
that detach these colonies
in a comfortable way, at a distance,
without having to scratch our hands.
The water that gave them life
removes their remains
with impersonal violence.

Now, it's almost always my brother who does this job:
he is very willing, and likes to work
with his hands, especially if it's on the boat.

Because of all his love for me,
he spares me the discomfort
of betraying my own laziness.

He throws off his winter scabbiness
and washes his sores
tearing apart the dirt of the hull
that slows down the thrust of his boat.

SI AIXÒ FOS UN CONTE

Si això fos un conte,
buscaria un lloc segur
per amagar el meu cor.

El posaria dins una maragda
amagada al niu d'una àguila
a la torre més alta d'un castell.

I el castell estaria en un país llunyà,
a moltes muntanyes, boscs i rius de distància.

Als camins hi hauria posat de guàrdia
llops i bruixes, gegants i dracs.

Sota cada pont viuria un troll,
amb un enigma per endevinar.

A cada bosc habitaria una fera,
intel·ligent com la fam.

Cada casa on passar la nit
seria un parany.

Cada tasca que acceptessis
una prova impossible.

Cada poma que et fos oferta
tendria un cuc a dins.

El castell fóra inexpugnable,
defensat per un exèrcit invicte.

I tot això seria inútil
perque les princeses com tu
sempre se surten amb la seva.

IF THIS WERE A FAIRY TALE

If this were a fairy tale
I would search for a safe place
to hide my heart in.

I would put it inside an emerald
hidden in an eagle's nest
on the highest tower of a castle.

And the castle would be in a distant land,
with lots of mountains, woods and rivers in between.

To guard the roads I would have set
wolves and witches, giants and dragons.

Under every bridge there would live a troll
with a riddle that had to be guessed.

In every wood there'd be a wild beast,
clever as hunger.

Every house, with its shelter for the night,
would be a trap.

Every task you might undertake
would be an impossible trial.

Every apple held out to yourself
would harbour a maggot.

The castle would be impregnable,
defended by a never-conquered army.

And all of this would be useless
because princesses like you
always come out on top.

MINERALS

He anat a comprar minerals
amb la Maria. Té set anys.

Els dissabtes hi ha un mercat de carrer
i un venedor que, a cops, en porta.

Hem arribat, les pedres
llueixen sota el sol. La meva filla
es ha anat tocant i triant
amb expressió de caçador.

Les pedres són més grosses
que la seva mà. Algunes són
més brillants que els seus ulls.

El firaire les assenyala:
- Aquesta és la pedra dels ulls,
aquesta és la pedra del cor,
aquesta té molta energia.

La meva filla el mira, seriosa,
i diu: – Això és una hematites,
això turquesa, això oliví,
això obsidiana nevada.

El posa al seu lloc. Poca broma.

Amb la mateixa cara seriosa
amb què tot sovint m'explica
que les fades existeixen;

que adesiara en veu.

MINERALS

I have come to buy minerals
with Maria. She is seven years old.

On Saturdays there is a street market
and a stall-holder who has some now and then.

We're here, the stones
gleam in the sun. My daughter
has begun lifting and choosing them
with the expression of a hunter.

The stones are bigger
than her hand. Some are
brighter than her eyes.

The stall-holder points at them:
– This is the stone of the eyes,
this is the stone of the heart,
this one is full of energy.

My daughter looks at him seriously,
and says: – That is a hæmatite,
that's a turquoise, that's olivine,
that is snowflake obsidian.

She puts him in his place.
It's not a joking matter.

And with the same serious expression
she wears when she often tells me
that fairies exist;

that from time to time she sees them.

ELS MILLORS AMICS

Vosaltres, amics meus, heu de saber
que mai no heu sigut els meus iguals.

La igualtat és sempre perillosa,
et fa pensar, et fa venir idees.
Un dia comences a cavil·lar
sobre aquesta dissortada entelèquia
i a l'altre dia et trobes, com si res,
deposant règims, guillotinant reis,
o justificant l'art conceptual.

No us diré pus mentides, ara basta:
vosaltres sou els meus millors amics
perque sé que sou millors que jo en tot.

BEST FRIENDS

You, my friends, should know
that you have have never been my equals.

Equality is always dangerous,
it makes you think, puts ideas in your head.
One day you start to brood
on this unfortunate entelechy
and before you know it you find yourself, just like that,
deposing régimes, chopping the heads off kings,
or justifying conceptual art.

I won’t tell you any more lies. That’s enough:
you are my best friends
because I know you are better than me in every way.

ELS IMPACTES MÍNIMS

Si un pensa en l'amor, pot passar
que s'imagini l'impacte d'una pedra
llençada per caprici per un soldat,
hores abans d'entrar en combat,
contra la superfícies d'un estany
i que vegi com del guèiser que hi neix
brollen ones concèntriques,
enormes inicialment i que disminueixen
la seva ambició a mesura que proven
d'abastar el món, i que vegi la seva mort
quan s'estavellen contra la riba.

I que es fixi també en els canvis
provocats en la riba per la mort
de les ones; en la terra remoguda,
en les plantes mullades,
en els trasbals dels insectes. Que pensi
en el destí del soldat. Potser traurà
conclusions sobre els efectes mínims;
sobre les conseqüències possibles
de l'impacte d'unes bales contra un cos,
de l'impacte d'un amor contra el món.

If a man thinks about love, it may be
that he imagines the impact of a stone
thrown on a whim by a soldier,
hours before going into battle,
at the surface of a pond
and he may see how, out of the geyser that spurts up,
there flow out concentric waves,
huge to begin with and which cause
his ambition to dwindle as they try
to reach the world, and he may see his death
when they break against the bank.

And say he focuses too on the changes
brought about on the bank by the death
of the waves; on the disturbed soil,
on the drenched plants,
on the struggling insects. He may ponder
the soldier's fate. Perhaps he will draw
conclusions on minimal effects;
on the possible consequences
of the impact of bullets on a body,
on the impact of one love on the world.

GENIUS LOCI

Són els veïns distants; una raça germana.
De sempre hem sabut que ens vigilen
repenjats comódament en els límits
de la nostra visió perifèrica.

Sabem també que no envelleixen,
i que som familia i que ja no ens feim.

Aquest distanciament és una de les raons
admeses del silenci sorneguer de Déu.

Fa anys els deixàvem regals
i menjar en els seus llocs preferits;
clarianes i entreforcs, sobretot.
Un dia hi varem posar creus de terme,
ermites i capelles. Varen haver de fugir.

Segur que ens ho tenen en compte
i que s'alimenten de les deixalles
que rebutjam. Com sempre, ens vetllen
sense acabar-s'ho de creure
i segueixen portant a terme
intercanvis i suplantacions.

Ens visiten i roben els cossos que escullen
com qui tria un vestit, i juguen amb nosaltres,
amb la casual crueltat quotidiana
pròpia dels germans majors.

I veig que t'han substituït,
que la persona que eres no és aquesta
que acaba de sortir de l'habitació.
La persona que ara em mira amb la cara transmudada
per la cocaïna i la metamfetamina

GENIUS LOCI

They are distant neighbours; a race of cousins.
We have always known that they keep watch on us
comfortably leaning against the boundaries
of our peripheral vision.

We know too that they never grow old,
and that we're related but are now no longer friends.

This rift is one of the reasons put forward
for the sly silence of God.

Years ago we would leave them gifts
and food in their favourite places;
clearings and crossroads, especially.
One day we set up boundary crosses there,
hermitages and chapels. They had to flee.

It's certain that they hold us responsible
and live off the leftovers
that we refuse. As ever, they keep watch on us
without ceasing to believe in it
and keep on carrying out
swappings and substitutions.
They visit us and steal the bodies that they choose
as one would select a dress, and they toy with us
with the casual everyday cruelty
common to older siblings.

And I see they have exchanged you,
that the person you were is not the one
who has just come out of the bedroom.

The one who now looks at me with a face utterly altered
by cocaine and methamphetamine

no ets tu, com ja no eres la persona
que vaig treure en braços del bany,
l'any passat, amb una xeringa
clavada a la vena d'adéu.

I sé que no tornaràs a ocupar el teu cos
fins a la pròxima crisi i que, al manicomi,
em culparàs de la teva reclusió
i intentaràs esgarrapar-me
la cara amb els teus bells dits d'esquelet,
esmolats i erms d'anells.

is not you, just as you are not the person
I carried in my arms out of the bathroom,
last year, with a syringe
stuck in the vein of goodbye.

And I know you will not return to occupy your body
until the next crisis and that, in the asylum,
you will blame me for being confined there
and you will try to scratch my face
with your beautiful skeletal fingers
sharpened and stripped of rings.

WATERLOO

The battle of Waterloo was won on the playing fields of Eton

Atribuït al Duc de Wellington

Érem petits. Sortíem a l'esplai
i procuràvem anar pels racons,
no ser evidents. Així aprenguérem
a fer-nos fonedissos amb el nostre
entorn. Mimetitzar-nos ens salvava
dels atacs, i ens donava, un dia més,
oportunitats de supervivència.

Creixérem i al pati vàrem aprendre
com formar escamots, com oferir
els més febles o lents d'entre nosaltres
com a sacrifici a la jerarquia
establerta de l'hora del esbarjo.

No vam poder amagar la pubertat
que ens va convertir en objectius a batre.
Així nosaltres passàrem a ser
els blancs principals del camp de batalla.

Férem dels racons més inaccesibles
de l'escola les nostres fortaleses
i observàrem, impotents, com alguns
traïdors d'entre nosaltres s'oferien
com a patges als majors i caçaven
per ells els desvalguts i els despistats.

Vaig veure sacrificis remarcables
i alguns actes de solidaritat.
Fins i tot algú es va fer capturar
per alleugerir el càstig d'un company
atrapat. Vaig veure com avançava
cap a les posicions enemigues

WATERLOO

The battle of Waterloo was won on the playing fields of Eton
Attributed to the Duke of Wellington

We were little. We came out into the open
and tried to keep to the corners,
to not stick out. Thus we learned
to make ourselves melt into
our background. Mimicking saved us
from being attacked and gave us, for one more day,
opportunities for survival.

We grew and in the playground we learned
how to form small squads, how to offer
the weakest or the slowest among us
as a sacrifice to the hierarchy
established at recreation-time.

We couldn't conceal puberty
which turned us into targets to be destroyed
And so we ourselves became
the main targets on the battle-field.

We turned the most inaccessible corners
of the school into our fortresses
and observed, powerless, how some
traitors among us offered themselves
as pages to the biggest and hunted down
for them the helpless and the bewildered.

I saw remarkable sacrifices
and some acts of solidarity.
Someone even had himself captured
to relieve the punishment of a companion
they had caught. I saw how he moved forwards
towards the enemy positions

amb els braços allargats als costats,
disposat a aprendre que violència
dividida per dos era igual
a violència multiplicada.

No es va respectar mai la valentia
en nosaltres; aviat vàrem veure
que els cops que David estavellà el roc
al front de Goliat, els filisteus
l'estomacaren per haver provat
de desobeir la llei del més fort.

Només vàrem triomfar en alguna
acció de guerrilla: algunes pedres
llençades per l'esquena o per mans
amagades entre la multitud
obriren el cap d'algun enemic.

Aprenguérem que podiem guanyar
qualque batalla, però que la guerra
estava perduda perque déu sempre
fa vèncer al bàndol que té més canons.

La batalla del temps d'esplai durà
fins que al darrer curs arribà per fi
el moment de la nostra hegemonia.

Ens havien ensinistrat per ser
els depredadors perfectes; taurons
sense oceà fabricats amb els cops
del martell pneumàtic amb el qual juga
l'evolució. Així ens cisellaren,
així ens formaren dia rere dia
per ser els estrategs definitius.

with his arms straight by his sides
ready to learn that violence
divided by two was equal
to violence multiplied.

There was never respect for any courage
we showed; we soon saw
that the times David smashed the stone
against Goliath's forehead, the Philistines
beat him up for having tried
to disobey the law of the strongest.

We only triumphed in some
guerrilla action: when a few stones
thrown at a back or by hands
concealed among the crowd
split open some enemy's head.

We learned that we could win
some battle or other, but that the war
was lost because God always
makes the side with the most guns win.

The battle of recreation-time lasted
until with the final class there came at last
the moment of our hegemony.

They had trained us to become
the perfect depredators: sharks
with no ocean made with the blows
of the pile-driver that evolution
plays with. In this fashion we were carved,
thus we were shaped day after day
to become the definitive strategists.

Alguns s'en sortiren, d'altres quedaren
afectats per fatiga de combat;
flashbacks traumàtics els feren reviure
durant anys les escenes on nosaltres
havíem sigut la pilota al mig
d'un rotlle indefugible de contraris.

Heu de saber que us recordo a tots
tant els executats com els botxins,
els que trobàreu honor en les derrotes
i els que, quan us vingué l'oportunitat,
escollíreu ser criminals de guerra.

Cada dia lluitàvem Waterloo
i succeïa amb l'aquiescència
d'uns religiosos, propietaris
de l'escola i els àrbitres absents
del conflicte (com els observadors
de l'ONU que analitzen els conflictes
des de les finestres del bar dels Hiltons
disseminats arreu del tercer món).

Encoratjaren amb la seva absència
la guerra que ens formaria el caràcter.

En el conflicte diari aprenguérem
a fer el paper d'emperadors caiguts.

Ensenyats com estam a ser els guerrers
més preparats en l'art de la derrota,
ara cada triomf sembla un miracle.

Some got out, others remained
affected by battle-fatigue;
traumatic flashbacks made them re-live
for years scenes where we
had been the ball in the middle
of an inevitable ring of opponents.

You should be aware that I remember you all,
the executed as well as the executioners,
those of you who found honour in defeat
and those who, when the opportunity arose,
would choose to carry out war-crimes.

Every day we fought our Waterloo
and it all went on with the acquiescence
of some religious, the owners
of the school and the referees absent
from the conflict (like the UN observers
who analyse conflicts
from the windows of bars in the Hiltons
scattered all over the third world).

They encouraged through their absence
the war that would build our character.

In the daily conflict we learned
to play the role of fallen emperors.

Taught as we were to be the best-prepared
warriors in the art of defeat,
every triumph now seems a miracle.

– Si t'ofereixen menjar no l'acceptis
– et diu la mare quan vas de visita.
– No malcontestis, saluda, no toquis.
Si et volen donar dolços pel carrer
digues que no i corre. No agafis mai
res de desconeguts. – També t'expliquen
els contes que no s'ha de tocar res
al país de les fades, que mai no
hi acceptis regals, que no hi mengis,
que pots dormir-hi cent anys o passar
a ser l'esclau que entregarà la Reina
de les Fades com tribut a l'infern,
el delme de carn de cada set anys.

Tot té el seu preu ocult. No hi regals.
Si en algun moment penses que podràs
esbrinar si estàs fent un bon negoci
o si t'estàs ensorrant; si t'ho sembla;
val més que et peguis un tir a la boca.

– If they offer you food, don't accept it –
your mother tells you when you're invited out.
– Don't be rude, say hello, but don't touch.
If anyone wants to give you sweets in the street
say no and run away. Don't ever take anything
from someone you don't know. – Fairy tales too
tell you how you mustn't touch anything
in fairyland, that you should never accept
gifts there, and never eat there,
or you might sleep for a hundred years, or become
the slave whom the Queen of the Fairies
will hand over as tribute to the devil,
the tithe of flesh every seven years.

Everything has its hidden price. There are no free gifts.
If at any time you think you'll be able
to find out whether you're pulling off a good deal
or whether they're putting one over you; if it looks like that
you'd be better off putting a gun in your mouth.

No t'enganyis, no volen escoltar
definicions de diccionari
que explicarien ben correctament
el gènere i algunes subtileses
prou adients a la qüestió.
Desitgen una resposta àgil, clara,
que els captivi un instant l'atenció.
Volen que expliquem, en un titular,
l'esperit del vi o la pinzellada
decisiva que pot acabar un quadre.

Que els expliquem amb paraules senzilles
(no més de quatre o cinc si pot esser)
la tragèdia d'Helena, la mort
d'Aquil·les, el viatge d'Odisseu,
els ulls d'Argos, l'espera de Penèlope
i tots els turqueses de la mar d'Ítaca.

Com veus és una missió molt fàcil
i per dur-la a terme hauràs de mentir
perquè ara saps del cert que poesia
només és el que restarà en nosaltres
molt després d'oblidar aquest poema.

Don't kid yourself, they don't want to listen
to dictionary definitions
that would explain perfectly correctly
the type of thing with a few subtleties
relevant enough to the question.
They want us to explain, in a headline,
the soul of wine or the decisive brushstroke
that can mean a painting is finished.

To explain to them in simple words
(not more than four or five if possible)
the tragedy of Helen, the death
of Achilles, the voyage of Odysseus,
the eyes of Argos, the waiting of Penelope
and all the shades of turquoise of the sea of Ithaca.

As you can see it's a very easy undertaking
and to bring it to fruition you'll have to lie
because you now know for sure that poetry
is only what is left inside us
long after forgetting this poem.

LA BIBLIOTECA SECRETA

Com els traços de la tinta que defineixen
el temps ocult, les temibles ratlles dels tigres
i els jeroglífics de les taques del jaguar
mostren l'escriptura d'un déu afeccionat
als astuts felins d'or i a la seva gràcia.

Al Puig de Randa, a Mallorca, Ramon Llull
desxifrava a les fulles de la *mata escrita*
cada dia les paraules verdes i grogues
dels capítols escrits per un déu botànic.

Se'ns ha revelat que el que busquem ens espera
als llibres muts d'una biblioteca secreta.

Podem començar a cercar la veritat
trobant on s'amaga la tinta que ens tatua
al món; l'escriptura breu d'esteles que ens ha
descrit a l'oceà. A la batalla que ens ha
estat promesa, al lloc d'avantguarda a què
se'ns destina abans de l'atac de l'enemic
o dins dels arxius d'un bibliotecari cec
trobarem les portes d'or, els panys i les claus
de la biblioteca secreta de l'oblit.

Like the traces of ink that define
hidden ages, the fearsome stripes of tigers
and the hieroglyphics of the jaguar's markings
show the writing of a god well-disposed
to clever golden felines and their grace.

At Puig de Randa, in Mallorca, Ramon Llull
deciphered every day on the pages of
the *thicket of writing* the green and yellow words
of chapters written by a botanical god.

It has been revealed that what we are searching for awaits us
in the dumb books of a secret library.

We can begin to search for the truth
by finding where the ink is hidden that tattoos us
in the world: the scant writing of the wakes left by boats, that have
described us in the ocean. In the battle that has
been promised us, at the place at the front to which
we are destined before the attack by the enemy
or in the archives of a blind librarian
we will find the golden doors, the locks and the keys
of oblivion's secret library.

EL SÒTIL

Havia d'anar amb compte. Cada passa ressonava
amb renou de buit i de temps. Les olors de menjar
de la cuina no arribaven tan amunt i jo gratava
entre andròmines i roba vella, assaborint les olors
del segó de les gallines i els fems i les parets humides
de cantó de Santanyí i mal ciment mallorquí.
Hi havia senalles de bova amb el cul foradat
i les decoracions de molts nadals en una discreta tenebra.

El sòtil era un petit món, jo el visitava d'amagat
per viure lluny del terra i les advertències dels majors.
La terra prohibida on hi havia els diaris d'anys
i una biblioteca groga de missals i Anys Cristians.

També hi havia els trofeus del padrí desconegut;
un cascavell de serp, un ou d'estruç, una armadura
d'armadillo, óssos innominats, restes d'un bestiari
fantàstic arribat de més enllà de la mar.

Molts dies, encara ara d'amagat, m'enfil al sòtil.
M'assec a un racó, amb els ulls tancats, ensum
la sentor de molsa, fems de gallina i bova vella.
Llegesc, gairebé sense llum, amb les mans tenyides
de pols groga, papers menjats per l'arna i peixos de plata.

I m'oblid que ja fa uns quants anys que l'esbucàrem.

THE ATTIC

You had to walk stealthily. Every footstep echoed,
disturbing emptiness and time. The smells of food
from the kitchen did not reach this high and I scrabbled
among lumber and old clothes, savouring the smells
of chicken bran and the dung and damp walls
of this corner of Santanyí and bad Mallorcan cement.
There were baskets made from bulrushes, bottoms stove-in,
and decorations from many Christmases in a tactful gloom.

The attic was a little world, and I visited it secretly
so as to be far from the ground and advice of the grown-ups.
The forbidden land where there were newspapers from years ago
and a yellow library of missals and The Christian Year.

There were also the trophies of an unknown godfather:
the rattle of a rattlesnake, an ostrich egg, the shell
of an armadillo, nameless bones, the remains of a fantastic
bestiary washed-up from across the seas.

Many days, still in secret now, I sneak up to the attic.
I sit in a corner, with my eyes closed, sniff out
the scent of moss, chicken-shit and old rushes.
With hardly any light, my hands stained by yellow dust,
I read papers eaten by moth and by silverfish.

And I forget that it's years since we demolished it.

BIOGRAPHICAL NOTES

Josep Lluís Aguiló (born Island of Mallorca, 1967) is a poet writing in the Catalan language. In 1986 he published his first collection of poems, *Cants d'arjau* (Songs from the Helm). After an interval of eighteen years, he published two further collections, *La biblioteca secreta* (The Secret Library) and *L'estació de les Ombres* (Season of Shadows), both in 2004.

His collection *Monstres* (Monsters, 2005) was awarded the Ciutat de Palma Joan Alcocer Poetry Prize in 2004 and, in 2006, the National Critics' Prize for the best book of poems written in Catalan – the Spanish Pulitzer – while it also received a Special Mention from the jury of the 2006 Poetry Prize of the Association of Catalan Writers.

In 2008, the present book, *Llunari* (Lunarium) was winner of the Jocs Florals de Barcelona Prize and Josep Lluís Aguiló was appointed Poet Laureate of the City of Barcelona during the period 2008-2009.

According to Pere Ballart in the preface of *Six Catalan Poets* (Arc Publications, 2013), the sequence formed by his four most recent books

> embraces a kaleidoscopic poetic adventure, that is culturalist in its symbols and in complete harmony with the eclecticism with which postmodernism juxtaposes the most learned and the most popular icons. In Aguiló's poetry, therefore, we find coexisting happily traditional rondeaux and the most bookish myths [...]

His poetry has appeared in several anthologies and has been translated into a number of languages.

ANNA CROWE, born in Plymouth in 1945, is a poet and translator and the author of four poetry collections in English: *Figure in a Landscape* (2010), a Poetry Book Society Choice which was translated into Catalan and published in a bilingual edition as *Paisatge amb figura* (Ensiola, 2011) and which also received the Callum MacDonald Memorial Award in 2011; *Skating Out of the House* (Peterloo, 1997), *A Secret History of Rhubarb* (2006), *Punk with Dulcimer* (Peterloo, 2006); one in Spanish / English bilingual edition: *L'ànima del teixidor* (Proa, 2000); and one in Catalan: *Punk con salterio,* translated by Joan Margarit (2008). She has translated three of Joan Margarit's collections: *Tugs in the Fog* (Bloodaxe, 2006, a Poetry Book Society Recommended Translation); *Barcelona, amor final* (Proa, 2007, Catalan / Castilian / English trilingual edition); *Strangely Happy* (Bloodaxe, 2011). She has also translated Anna Aguilar-Amat's *Música i escorbut* (Blesok, 2006); with Iolanda Pelegrí, an anthology of Catalan poetry, *Miralls d'aigua* (*Light Off Water,* Scottish Poetry Library / Carcanet Press, 2006); and, for Arc Publications *Six Catalan Poets* edited by Pere Ballart (2013) and *Peatlands: Selected Poems* by Pedro Serrano (2014).

Along with several other writers, she was a founder member of StAnza, the Scottish international poetry festival, and was artistic director during its first seven years. She has twice won the Peterloo Open Poetry competition, and in 2005 was awarded a travelling scholarship from the Society of Authors.

Arc Publications
publishes translated poetry in bilingual editions
in these series:

ARC TRANSLATIONS
Series Editor Jean Boase-Beier

'VISIBLE POETS'
Series Editor Jean Boase-Beier

ARC CLASSICS:
NEW TRANSLATIONS OF GREAT POETS OF THE PAST
Series Editor Jean Boase-Beier

ARC ANTHOLOGIES IN TRANSLATION
Series Editor Jean Boase-Beier

NEW VOICES FROM EUROPE & BEYOND
(anthologies)
Series Editor Alexandra Büchler

details of which can be found on the
Arc Publications website at
arcpublications.co.uk